my first fruits
in modern greek

translated by Lydia Kopanou

polyglot kids

μήλο

MEE-loh

apple

αχλάδι

akh-LAH-thee

pear

σταφύλι

stah-FEE-lee

grape

σύκο

SEE-koh

fig

μούρο

MOO-roh

mulberry

δαμάσκηνο

thah-MAH-skee-noh

plum

κεράσι

keh-RAH-see

cherry

ροδάκινο

roh-THAH-kee-noh

peach

ρόδι

ROH-thee

pomegranate

πεπόνι

peh-POH-nee

melon

© 2025 by Polyglot Kids Books / World Poetry Books
Photography © 2025 by Sebastian Fröhlich

Series editors: Peter Constantine & Hannes Schumacher
Translated into Modern Greek by Lydia Kopanou
Photography: Sebastian Fröhlich
Design: Hannes Schumacher & Sebastian Fröhlich
ISBN: 978-1-967821-10-5

Polyglot Kids Books is an imprint of World Poetry Books, Inc. New York.

www.ingramcontent.com/pod-product-compliance
Lightning Source LLC
Chambersburg PA
CBHW062022050526
44107CB00106B/944